Oh, Mawson, What if ..

I'm not being Me

Right?

Who <u>is</u> "Me", really?

You know, Frilly, how, sometimes
you feel like you're in a Story
that someone's telling ?

Perhaps, your "Me" is Who's listening.

Couldn't I be Who's Telling it ?

Then I'd make me different.

Such big Questions.

Has something upset you, Frilly?

Well, Mawson, you see, I … umm … ran away.

You ran away? From

L O V E?

It shone so

Brightly

I was scared.

I want to become a Me who's brave.

So I'm going ... Oh dear ...

on a Quest.

I've just the thing - shining armour.
And a noble steed, perhaps?

But

they're

not

Pink.

Oops.

Besides, it's a quiet sort of Quest.

Frilly, why not Quest at home ?

Lots of Journeys go
to Where one's Sitting.

But I want to boldly

Find My Self.

Here's a Hug to take with you, Frilly.

I hope I don't
have far to go.

I must be brave.

I will be brave.

I
might
find
what
I want

..

.. on a
mountain
top.

Bother. This one's taken.

Onward!

That's what bold Questers say.

Shoo! Shoo! I hope they say that too.

I won't give up now.

At last.

Hello there ... errr .. Me. It's me, Frilly.
Why, hello, Frilly, It's <u>Me</u> here too.
Being <u>You</u>."

Oh? Are you? Well, hello to <u>You</u> .. err no,
I mean hello ME ... Hmmmm ... So ...
Here ... I ... Am.

Hmmm ... Let's try ...   "They who go
Alone and quietly,
Who seek to to be their best,
They go on the grandest quest".

What happened to the hug
I gave you, Frilly ?

It wore off.

And did you find Your Self?

Yes, Mawson. But ...

Tedette
Kleening

... There's no one else to play with
when you get there.

Oh, Mawson. Will I ever find Happiness?

Happiness. Hmmmm. Let me see ...

Umm ... Find? ... No.

But you can Be it sometimes.

Be Happiness?

Let's practise it.

Here, Frilly, **p a i n t** how you feel.

I call it, "Even the Rain
Weeps Songs of Sorrow".

Oh.

While I'm being sad, Mawson,
can I just sit with you?

We can Hum as we sit.

It's another kind of practice.

Let the paws fall ... Go floppy all over ...

And ... Ahuuummmmmmmmmmmm

Ahuuummmmmmmmmmmmmmmmmm

Gently notice ... Ahmmmmmmm ... Whatever
may present itself to you ...hmmmmmm ...

Mawson, look! Honey-Choco-Mello-Creams!

<u>Except</u> honey-choco-mello-creams.
And now ... ahummmmmmmm ... plumping up
our stuffing ... hmmmmmm ... we feel like
we are in the middle of our ... umm ...
of our Middles ... errr, Frilly? Frilly?

Or, in the Middle of a Dream.

I'll just write and ponder things
'till she wakes.

Oh, Mawson, I felt like a balloon floating up

Then I reached out ...
and I nearly ... touched ...

N O T H I N G

But ... it wasn't There.
So I didn't.

It's no use, Mawson.
My Story's still going all wrong.

Your Story, Frilly?

Here, why don't <u>you</u> tell it.

The way I want to ?

These words look glad to be written.
Frilly, you're good at this.

I am? Why, yes. I am.
It feels ... Right.

Look! The LIGHT
of LOVE

It's come
back for
you, Frilly.

So
bright

Still
scared?

Yes.

But ...

I'm Going In.

She's wanted.

She's ready.

She's gone.

While I'm being glad ... and sad ...

I'll just sit with me.

Mail, Mawson.